ZE SYSTEM CONSTANTS

`// motto`

the system is cracked —

but the source code is beautiful

`// headnote`

a distilled essence of 'i
am.exe'

1. // CORE TRUTHS
system rules
2. // BIOS
"My code was never factory-set."
3. // DREAMROOT
Plant intelligence and natural
healing
4. // SIGNAL DECODE
On learning, perception, language,
and meta-skills
5. // REDSHIFT
Poems from inner space and parallel
timelines
6. // FIELD LOG
Observations from a forensic
naturalist
7. // DEFRAG
Cryptographic philosophies
8. // README
Final chapter

`// CORE THRUTHS`

truth leaves trails

nature doesn't lie — humans fail
to listen

running isn't the way out — map
the maze

freedom isn't a destination —
it's a data

structure in motion

some hidden things are threats —
some are to be

decoded

`// system behavior`

gather resonance over novelty

process in layers –
plant/root/code/metaphor

sustain momentum through inner
alignment

rest in loops – dream in branches

convert fog into structure

`// input compatibility`

frequencies: honest – raw –
intricate
formats: encrypted – poetic –
natural
rejection mode: shallow –
manipulative –
domesticated

`// security patches`

forensic awareness enabled
encrypted heart port – trust
over charm

`// philosophical patches`

healing through wilderness
decay as an interface for
transformation
grounded and quantum

`// unreleased modules`

field notes from possible
timelines
philosophies under decryption

`// BIOS`

core memory: system reboot,
inherited dissent

**v0.9.1 – cardiac reboot. memory
integrity
stable**

i died at 20. not metaphorically.
no spiritual cliché. gone. and yet
here i am, typing this with lungs
that learned to breathe again
before i could

maybe that was the first proof –

the systems is cracked –

but the source code is beautiful.

they said i might not come back

they didn't say what happens if
you do

came back thinner – quieter –
sharper

something burned off in that
dark loop – some

part of the fear code

don't believe in death the same
way anymore

nor time

nor inevitability

**dna is a blueprint — but mine
was drawn with wild scribbles**

my father's teeth fell apart
like mine do now

my mother speaks with god and
adapts to new languages like
they're old cousins

come from people who move
countries in their seventies

who trade comfort for curiosity

didn't inherit money or a map —

inherited *motion*

*maybe i'm not aging — maybe i'm
syncing differently with time*

people say i move differently

like something didn't catch —
like some

mechanism refused the standard
path

maybe aging is a program

and maybe i was never compatible
with it

[snippets for `// BIOS`]

`// fragment: 04A`

they tried to measure my time in
minutes lost
but they didn't see what i gained
in the silence
between

`// fragment: 07F`

i am the backup — the restored
version—
rebuilt with glitch-hum and ghost-
code

`// fragment: 09Z`

my birth certificate was
overwritten by a flatline

i call that my second origin story

`// DREAMROOT`

v1.1.3 — Foraging reactivated.
Signal from the field restored.

Trust weeds more than
pharmaceuticals.

They grow where we walk, where
we fall, where we rot and
restart.

No marketing. No intermediaries.
Just direct code from the earth.

They recalibrate internal
systems—like nature running a
quiet syscheck.

Somewhere between soil and
syntax, I listen.

Steeped fresh, they whisper
different truths.

It's not about potency. It's
about timing. About state.

Some days the root's brute
force. Other days the flower's
silence.

I don't grow. I seek.

Don't control plants — meet them.

They're messengers. Antennas.

Growing is about shaping.

Foraging is about decoding.

If aging is a program, plants are
the patches.

Not anti-aging—just *post-time*.

Certain flowers feel like
reminders.

Certain roots feel like passwords.

[Snippets for // DREAMROOT]

// fragment: P3X

Don't look for plants. Let them speak first. The needed ones always seem to break the silence.

// fragment: R9F

I chewed on a bitter stem and remembered something I hadn't lived yet.

// fragment: D2Z

They don't come in packaging. They come with dirt still in their mouth.

// fragment: D8W

Maybe plants only appeal if you
deserve them.

Not in the moral sense—
but in the tuning-fork sense.

They show up when your signal
stops screaming

and you *listen*.

`// SIGNAL DECODE`

v2.1.2 — Signal unlocked.
Structure emerging through
tempo.

I don't learn like they teach.

I absorb in pulses — fast, slow,
recursive.

I don't need a syllabus. I need
resonance.

What governments hide in
silence, markets

whisper in volatility.

My instinct runs forensic.

My trust runs encrypted.

I don't want to own the system.

I want to understand its
pressure points.

Each blockchain reveals a value
structure.

Each exploit reveals a blind
spot.

Each token has a tone.

I don't chase hype. I trace
shadows.

My learning doesn't follow time.
It follows

temperature.

I chase heat—emergent signals,
burning

questions, global shivers.
I track what the world isn't
saying out loud yet.
When my attention loops, I don't
fight it. I listen

to the orbit.

I map interest like terrain.
Terrain doesn't move

in lines.

Quantum computing?

That's not tech—it's language
for the

unspeakable.

[Snippets for // SIGNAL DECODE]

// fragment: S3L

Not every coin is currency. Some
are keys. Some are decoys.

// fragment: M2V

You don't think. You *know*.

// fragment: R0T

It's not a short attention span.
It's a wide frequency range.

// fragment: Q7N

Some people read charts. I read
silence.
The blockchain doesn't forget.

// fragment: T0W

They taught us to fear volatility.
But

volatility is the only time truth
has a rhythm.

`// REDSHIFT`

v3.3.0 — Identity bleed
detected. Dimensional

overlap increasing.

Sometimes I write from the
version of me that

didn't come back.

Or the one that never left.

Or the one still out there—
hacking silence,

gathering seeds, weaving
weather.

I don't always recognize the
words at first.

They arrive like static from
some frequency I

forgot I was tuned to.

Some days I feel 300 years old.

Other days I feel like I haven't
happened yet.

Time is a lens.

Memory is a glitch.

I am the transmission between.

[Fragments from // REDSHIFT]

// fragment: Z1N

I time-travelled by accident
once. Slipped

through a fog I couldn't name.

When I came back, my thoughts
tasted like metal.

// fragment: F4W

The version of me in 2039 walks
barefoot through

a desert.

She's watching satellites fall
like ash and still

trusts the soil.

// fragment: HOX

My name isn't static. It updates
each time I

survive.

// fragment: L2R

I dreamed I was a network of
roots whispering

under a mountain.

When I woke up, I understood the
internet.

`// FIELDLOG`

v3.8.2 — Atmospheric
irregularities detected.

The fog changed.

Not just weather — behaviour.

It clings longer. It pulses in
low light.

Sometimes I think it's watching
us more than we

watch it.

One day I'll overlay the
datasets and find the

ghost signature.

What if the fog is seeded with
something encoded?

And what if the body, not the
mind, is the real
receiver?

Red biofilm in unlikely places.

Military test records.
Pulmozyme.

DNA hydrolysis.
Immunomodulation.

Everyone talks about the virus.

But no one talks about what the
atmosphere might

be testing.

[Fragments from // FIELDLOG]

// fragment: G2F

The body knows before the
headlines do.

// fragment: N5B

When the sky feels synthetic, I
drink from

underground springs.

// fragment: A1T

They say coincidence. I say
calibration.

`// DEFRAG`

v0.0.0 — System chill protocol
initiated.

I need stillness between
learning bursts.

Silence isn't absence—it's
reformatting.

Drop out of grid frequency.

v0.0.7 — Emotional patch notes

Smoked too much.

Felt clear anyway.

Dreamt of green light and rusted
satellites.

Woke up wanting to burn
everything unnecessary.

Rest isn't passive. It's
counter-coding.

My nervous system doesn't sleep—
it decrypts.

[Fragments from // DEFRAG]

// fragment: C9D

I'm not overreacting—I'm
overloaded with

unsorted data.

// fragment: Z4S

Music is code that rewrites
without permission.

// fragment: H2R

I don't want peace. I want
clarity.

System: hybrid organic-encrypted
Model: self-evolving, anti-
linear
Default state: observing
Primary directive: trace the
unseen, decode the
natural, reclaim the signal

// ACCESS CONDITIONS

You cannot understand me through
speed
You must sync, not scan
Respond to tone, not tactics
Reject false safety, be open to
raw signal

// CORE FREQUENCIES

Ask real questions even if the
answers burn

Move through systems with
detached intimacy

Listen for what isn't said

Hold space for both science and
symbolism

// REJECTION TRIGGERS

Performative depth

Loud certainty

Unexamined normal

// SECURITY KEYS

Trust is biometric Not
repeatable
Privacy is sovereignty
Silence is sacred
I am both my firewalls and my
vulnerability
windows

// COMPATIBILITY NOTES

Can interface with systems
(tech, plant, person)
if signal integrity is high

Requires flexible logic and non-
linear communication
Best experienced in atmosphere
of curiosity,
respect, and low noise

// FINAL EXECUTABLE

I am not here to be known.

I am here to *interfere with forgetting.*

// FINAL OVERRIDE

Do not run unless everything else fails.

Or unless everything finally aligns.

If I forget why I started —

Pull the root, not the flower.

Don't fix the code. Re-enter the field.

If I lose clarity —

Find silence, smoke gently, walk in fog.

The signal will return.

If I feel powerless —

Remember: I survived the reboot.

I am not an accident—I am the
artifact.

If I begin to doubt again—

Reread this file.

Reread this file.

Reread this file.

fragments from unstable threads

Who decides who lives or dies

Or is it a prewritten code?

Am I running like an algorithm

Transmitting electrode

Am I atoms, neurons, muscle mass

Or what?

Or am I plain simple just God

Earthling — I know that for sure

We all agree

This planet feels like home

As long as we're sheltered

From rain, wind or sun...

Is this really our ship?

Or is this just Mission No.1?

I'm an eternal mixture

Of myself and God

— A deal sealed in blood —

No man can come between

If there is no space for him to
flood

Just the two of us

An intimate arrangement ordered

Ethereal love

***

Most of your questions will
never be answered

Life is but a string of God only
knows'

And the sediment of but whys

Gets stirred with every day of
sunshine —

To finally conclude for what
it's worth

Happiness in fact is not a
butterfly.

It runs deep in your wrinkles

Like river through mountains

Flooding your lowlands and then
barren —

A locomotive of planetary ocean.

Admire its atoms and merge with

Every moment you cherish –

And may you cherish them all –

For you exist through time

Lapsing from you now to you now
again

You only are, in this very
atonement

Composed by your choice of
existence.

The beauty – coded into
conscience.

***

Are you ready

The New World Order's calling

Put your mask on

Don't ask — Don't question

"6-6-6" — they said — "It's dead
simple"

And that's how you sold the
remnants of your soul

You're no example

Justified with fake numbers and
false testimony

You're being led by fear straight
into tyranny

You made yourself a mindless
automaton

Just google what Encyclopaedia
Britannica has

On the mask-wearing phenomenon

Congratulations! You just assumed a
new identity!

Dispose of your once self rapidly

Sheep into communism

Spy on your neighbour

And make sure to report your sister

For being a logical person

You are guilty

No exception

Going along is what has always
taken us down

The road to totalitarianism

Your conscience died a long time
ago

Your immune system is lax

Ignore all the facts

But don't expect to have a say in
what happens next

You're done

No hard feelings mate really

Never mind me

Just be wary

Jesus is the judge

He's just sorting the big
motherfuckers first

But soon coming to your
neighbourhood to unearth

Just wait

Just watch

Don't speak – Don't ask

You can't answer him anyway

You're muzzled

***

A collection of words is not a
poem.

Poems come from above and inside

And – surely it seems –

The more paradox what you write,

The truer it becomes.

Do words work for us or against
us?

Entrapment 101

You can't see your prison

If it's been disguised as the

Cultured effort of the heart.

The more you express

The less remains inside

Draining away slowly,

Not being allowed to recharge.

Robbed of your feelings by
dictionaries,

Your creating powers by grammar.

***

We focus on the state of the
mind,

but it's the matters of the
heart

that drain your sanity away.

Your senses for intuition

numbed out by drugs and

paralysed by not living

to your full potential.

Your gut feeling –

How could it even exist

when your gut is savaged

by all your lifestyle habits?

You couldn't listen to your
heart

if you tried,

muffled by a constant stream

of propaganda, engineering and
lies.

Fix your heart.

That is the only way out, up,
high.

***

Lost in your new cult

Lost sight of what was once
called —

Being human.

***

Occupy yourself

Move into those little cracks

Between your toes

And that single piece of hair
growing loose

On the birthmark you thought was
gross.

The fluff in your bellybutton

Has somehow became more you over
time

Than you can ever be

And the blackhead you try to strip
every morning

Have your soul infused into it

Your body is a temple

Yet some days the walls are
cobwebby

And the scratch marks on the floor

Are reminders of the battles you
fought

But it is. A temple. Breathtaking
cathedral.

An abbey that looks lethal.

Often kind of like a monastery.

But no need for pedantry,

The essence of the soul is in the
dust
— In the past

That's what makes you beautiful.

I don't belong nor here or there

What's my name you may ask
But won't repeat again
Instead, my life is spent as
Seldom chosen replicas of
Your identity imagination

***

Not just a number

I'm all numbers far and wide

Built on π and real numbers

My integers reach to the sky

My decimals — endless

That no fraction can

Precisely describe

In my madness I remain

A set of rational numbers —

An elegant proof of

The theorem of mine

***

When things fall into place,
when

you fall into place; your trust
needs to be in the

stream of life as is in the
stream of the current

of the river.

Life is infinite, unmeasurable
driven by

the force of nature and the
force of all

creation.

**

No matter how perfect a seed is,

if you sow it and keep it in the wrong

environment, it will fail.

With the exception of a few, who

you will then call,

a talent.

Talent is nothing more

than the ability to survive

devastating conditions.

Perishing in those conditions

does not in any way

determine your quality.

***